CHICAGO

2016

The Food Enthusiast's Complete Restaurant Guide

Sebastian Bond

Sebastian Bond is the Food Enthusiast.
When he's not playing tennis,
he dines anonymously
at the Publisher's expense.

Gramercy Park Press
New York – London - Paris

Please submit corrections, additions or comments to
gppress@gmail.com

Chicago
2016

The Food Enthusiast's
Complete Restaurant Guide

Table of Contents

Introduction

What a wonderful town, Chicagoland.

I couldn't believe the place when I first saw it. I was coming from New York (back in the '70s) in fine weather in early summer. It was night. I took a cab into town and walked up the Magnificent Mile in awe. Ladies and gentlemen walked down the street arm-in-arm, actually promenading.

There was grass on Michigan Avenue. Real grass. I reached down and touched it. You wouldn't find grass like that on Fifth Avenue. No, sir.

There was an electricity in the air in Chicago I noticed that very first night. And I've always been aware of it. There's that same sense in New York, of course, a sensation of excitement, of swiftness, of opportunity—*of hustle*—but somehow it was different here in Chicago. The pace here has slightly less of an edge to it. The people are nicer. They are polite. They are not rude, crude or rough. Maybe the word I'm looking for is *Normal*. It's that Midwest upbringing, I tell myself, and that must be it. This may be the City of Big Shoulders, but the people inhabiting it are as nice as the farmers plowing fields

300 miles away. (Well, there are certain neighborhoods….)

    That first night I spent sleeping on the floor of our branch office at the corner of Oak and Rush, which I found out later was quite an exciting corner with a fascinating history. When I woke up in the morning and looked out of the floor-to-ceiling windows, I saw people swimming in the lake.

Swimming!
In the lake. In the 1970s!
I was aghast.

Back in New York, you wouldn't dip your toe in the Hudson River or the East River.

That was then. This is now. Now they're harvesting oysters from beds in the East River.

I remember running down and asking a cop how people could swim in the filthy water. He explained that the river flowing into the lake had been reversed. The river flowed *backwards!* The water was clean.

I couldn't believe it.

But this was just the beginning of a long love affair with Chicago. There's nothing not to like about this town—except the freezing wind that comes off the lake in the wintertime.

A couple of years later, in February, I was having a business lunch at the top of the **Hancock Tower** in what is now called the **Signature Room**. A blizzard blew snow off the lake so hard the snow moved horizontally, not vertically. Looking over the shoulder of the person opposite me, I saw the building swaying. I didn't know if the Hancock Tower was swaying or the building I was looking at. I am not an engineer. I just knew this was no place for a Southern boy.

After lunch, my head bent down, I made my way back to my office and announced to the staff that the Editorial Department of our travel magazine (that would be me) was moving to our offices in Miami, at least for the winter months.

I've returned dozens of times, of course—even in February—and the simple truth is that whether it's winter, summer, spring or fall, there's no place like this Toddlin' Town.

Before we get into the nitty-gritty, I'm reprinting Carl Sanders's famous poem "Chicago," first published I think in 1914. It captures the city like no other verse ever written.

HOG Butcher for the World,
    Tool Maker, Stacker of Wheat,
    Player with Railroads and the Nation's Freight Handler;
    Stormy, husky, brawling,
    City of the Big Shoulders:
    They tell me you are wicked and I believe them, for
    I have seen your painted women under the gas lamps
        luring the farm boys.
And they tell me you are crooked and I answer: Yes, it
    is true I have seen the gunman kill and go free to
    kill again.
And they tell me you are brutal and my reply is: On the
    faces of women and children I have seen the marks
    of wanton hunger.
And having answered so I turn once more to those who
    sneer at this my city, and I give them back the

sneer
    and say to them:
Come and show me another city with lifted head
singing
    so proud to be alive and coarse and strong and
cunning.
Flinging magnetic curses amid the toil of piling job
on
    job, here is a tall bold slugger set vivid against the
    little soft cities;
Fierce as a dog with tongue lapping for action,
cunning
    as a savage pitted against the wilderness,
        Bareheaded,
        Shoveling,
        Wrecking,
        Planning,
        Building, breaking, rebuilding,
Under the smoke, dust all over his mouth, laughing
with
    white teeth,
Under the terrible burden of destiny laughing as a
young
    man laughs,
Laughing even as an ignorant fighter laughs who has
    never lost a battle,
Bragging and laughing that under his wrist is the
pulse.
    and under his ribs the heart of the people,
            Laughing!
Laughing the stormy, husky, brawling laughter of
    Youth, half-naked, sweating, proud to be Hog
    Butcher, Tool Maker, Stacker of Wheat, Player

with
   Railroads and Freight Handler to the Nation.

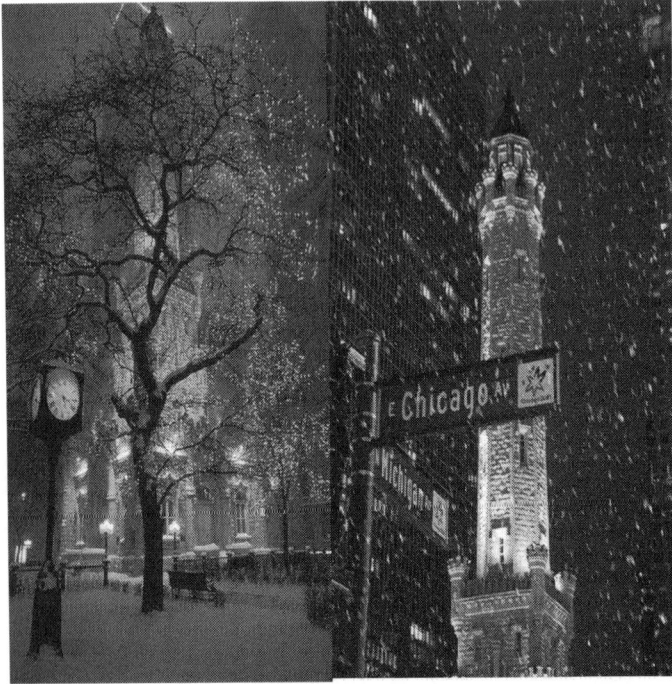

   There are so many different worlds in Chicago.
There are the edgier sections of Pilsen and Logan
Square, the old city center in the Loop, the dramatic
sweep of buildings along the Gold Coast fronting a
beach that in summertime looks almost like it doesn't
belong here, the Puerto Rican barrios of Humboldt
Park and Devon Avenue, the elegant areas around
Hyde Park, the craziness of Boystown, the world-
class shopping along the Magnificent Mile, the
theatre scene that's second only to what you'll find in
New York, a music scene that's among the most

vibrant in the country, you will find it almost impossible to absorb all this glorious city has to offer over a Long Weekend.

But you will get a taste so thrilling that you'll want to return again and again.

The A to Z Listings

2 SPARROWS
553 W Diversey Pkwy, Chicago, 773-234-2320
www.2sparrowschicago.com
CUISINE: American
DRINKS: Full Bar
SERVING: Breakfast, Lunch
PRICE RANGE: $$
NEIGHBORHOOD: Lincoln Park
This is one of Chicago's favorite brunch spots and there's always a wait on the weekend. For breakfast/brunch you'll be treated to old favorites with a twist – like the cinnamon roll with goat cheese icing and pancetta instead of Canadian bacon on the Eggs Benedict. Chef Gregory Ellis offers a menu of American comfort fare featuring ingredients from

local farmers, artisans, and brew masters. Delicious brunch cocktails and craft beer pairings.

ANN SATHER
929 W Belmont Ave, Chicago, 773-348-2378
www.annsather.com
CUISINE: Scandinavian
DRINKS: No Booze
SERVING: Breakfast, Brunch
PRICE RANGE: $$
NEIGHBORHOOD: Lakeview
One of several scattered throughout Chicago, this Swedish eatery serves up one of the best breakfasts in town. Menu favorites include: Swedish Breakfast and once you taste one of their fresh-baked cinnamon rolls, you'll rave about them too.

ARCADIA
1639 S Wabash Ave, Chicago, 312-360-9500
www.acadiachicago.com

CUISINE: American
DRINKS: Full Bar
SERVING: Dinner
PRICE RANGE: $$$$
NEIGHBORHOOD: Near Southside/South Loop
Run by Chef Ryan McCaskey, this high-end eatery offers a creative menu featuring dishes like Lobster potpie and Black cod. If you're a meat lover, try the Wagu tri-tip, a meat and potatoes dish with thick slices of beef. Desserts are just as interesting and delicious especially the chocolate pudding that's filled with pieces of sponge cake, hazelnuts, and almond-cookie shards. The bar serves novel cocktails and offers a nice wine list. The décor is simple but comfortable. Closed Monday and Tuesday.

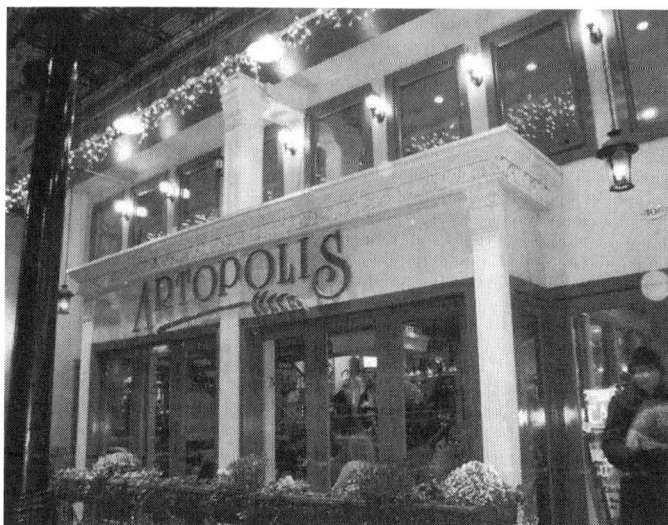

ARTOPOLIS BAKERY & CAFE
306 S Halsted St, Chicago, 312-559-9000

www.artopolischicago.com
CUISINE: Greek
DRINKS: Full Bar
SERVING: Brunch, Lunch, Dinner
PRICE RANGE: $$
NEIGHBORHOOD: Near West Side
A combination bakery, café, bar and retail shop. Here you'll find fresh baked Greek pastries like their signature "artopitas." Their menu features a selection of soups, salads, wood-fired pizzas and sandwiches made with hearth-baked bread. Traditional Greek dishes like eggplant moussaka and roasted leg of lamb are also offered. In the shop you'll find breads and pastries, gift baskets, chocolates, olive oils and vinegars.

ATWOOD CAFÉ
1 W Washington St, Chicago, 312-368-1900
www.atwoodcafe.com

CUISINE: American
DRINKS: Full Bar
SERVING: Breakfast, Lunch, Dinner
PRICE RANGE: $$$
NEIGHBORHOOD: The Loop
Located in the historic Reliance Building along with the **Hotel Burnham**, this restaurant offers classic American cuisine served in an Art Deco decorated dining room that features 18-foot-tall windows. Chef Derek Simcik's menu features dishes made with fresh, seasonal ingredients. Menu favorites include: Roasted chicken and Vegetable pot pie. Great choice for pre-theater nosh.

AVEC
615 W Randolph St, Chicago, 312-377-2002
www.avecrestaurant.com
CUISINE: French/Mediterranean

DRINKS: Full Bar
SERVING: Dinner; brunch on weekends
PRICE RANGE: $$$
NEIGHBORHOOD: Near West Side
This "intimate" restaurant offers a small plate menu
and communal seating. It's a little Spartan for my
taste (no backs on the bar stools, etc.), and I defy you
to conjure up a more minimal décor. Menu favorites
include Ricotta flatbread, Pork shoulder and
Papperdelle. No reservations – which means there's
often a wait.

BALENA
1633 N Halsted St, Chicago, 312-867-3888
www.balenachicago.com
CUISINE: Italian
DRINKS: Full Bar
SERVING: Dinner
PRICE RANGE: $$$
NEIGHBORHOOD: Lincoln Park
With Chef Chris Pandel at the helm, this restaurant
offers a menu of "honest, Italian cooking" that
includes impressive pizzas, delicious pastas, and an
outstanding wine list. Menu favorites include:
Smoked mackrel, Fresh salmon and Sea Urchin pasta.
Great choice for pre-theatre dining.

BELLY Q
1400 W Randolph St, Chicago, 312-563-1010
www.bellyqchicago.com
CUISINE: Asian Fusion, Barbeque
DRINKS: Full Bar
SERVING: Dinner, Brunch

PRICE RANGE: $$$
NEIGHBORHOOD: Near West Side
A comfortable restaurant with a rustic yet modern
décor offering a creative menu. Menu favorites
include: Goat Milk Feta Panake, Wood Grilled
Chicken wit Peanut Noodle Salad, and Sticky Rice
with Shrimp Togarashi, Chinese Sausage and
Mushrooms. Portions are large so you'll probably
leave with a doggie-bag. Ideal place for a date.

BERGHOFF
17 W Adams St, Chicago, 312-427-3170
www.theberghoff.com
CUISINE: German
DRINKS: Full Bar
SERVING: Lunch, Dinner
PRICE RANGE: $$
NEIGHBORHOOD: The Loop

A Chicago landmark, this restaurant serves German-style cuisine offering a variety of appetizers, salads, sandwiches, and entrees including vegetarian and gluten-free dishes. Menu favorites include: Weiner Schnitzel and Jagerschnitzel - Pork Cutlet, with mushrooms and bacon. Good selection of German beer and lagers.

BIG STAR
1531 N Damen, (bet. Wicker Park Ave & Pierce Ave), Chicago, 773-235-4039
www.bigstarchicago.com
CUISINE: Mexican, Tex-Mex
DRINKS: Full Bar
SERVING: Lunch, Dinner & Late Night
PRICE RANGE: $$
NEIGHBORHOOD: Wicker Park

Nice range of Mexican food, from fish, chicken and beef tacos, to a Sonoran Hot Dag (a bacon-wrapped hot dog with pinto beans, lime mayo, mustard, onions and Big Star hot sauce on a bolillo roll). Most people don't know it, but Big Star has blended 20+ signature barrels of whiskey with some of Kentucky's best distilleries, creating perhaps the biggest single-barrel selection in the U.S. If you like American whiskey, you MUST put a stop here at the top of your list.

BILLY GOAT TAVERN
430 N Michigan Ave (Lower Level), Chicago, 312-222-1525
www.billygoattavern.com
CUISINE: American, Burgers
DRINKS: Full Bar
SERVING: Lunch & Dinner
PRICE RANGE: $
NEIGHBORHOOD: Near North Side
Located underneath the Chicago Tribune Building, this tavern offers a genuine diner/soda fountain feel. Worth a stop if you're in the neighborhood but other than that the burgers aren't that impressive. Locations all over the city.

BLACKBIRD
619 W Randolph St, Chicago, 312-715-0708
www.blackbirdrestaurant.com
CUISINE: American
DRINKS: Full Bar
SERVING: Lunch & Dinner
PRICE RANGE: $$$
NEIGHBORHOOD: Near West Side

They can claim Michelin stars here since 2011, and the cooks here (sorry, chefs) have more James Beard Awards than you can shake a stick at. I find the décor to be antiseptic and clinically sleek and modern, to the point that the bar looks like a big white slab on which a medical examiner might conduct an autopsy. It's about as warm and fuzzy and charming in here as a meat locker. But if you look past the studied modernity of the setting, you'll love the food: roasted chicken roulade, hanger steak with rutabaga (I love rutabaga, and you so seldom see it offered), wood-grilled sturgeon with roasted leeks, sucking pig served with risotto (dinner only), poached turbot (the most delicate I've had in a long time), and the aged duck breast, simply outstanding.

BREAD & WINE
3732 W Irving Park Rd, (between Hamlin & Ridgeway Aves), Chicago, 773-866-5266

www.breadandwinechicago.com
CUISINE: American
DRINKS: Full Bar
SERVING: Lunch & Dinner
PRICE RANGE: $$$
NEIGHBORHOOD: Irving Park
A farm-to-table bistro with terrific Roman-style semolina gnocchi and grass-fed burgers. That being said, I'd focus on the delectable house-made charcuterie platters here: chicken liver pate, country ham, mortadella, summer blood sausage, BBQ chicharron, Kielbasa, Tasso ham and pork rillettes. The small shop in the front provides solid picnic fixings with good, affordable wines, small-batch preserves and the restaurant's own line of whole-grain granola, biscotti and other goods. Even the chips they sell are made locally. Eggplant spread, McClure's pickles, artisanal olive oils, vinegars and salt, seasonally changing array of local or unique beers, lots more. Obviously, this is a great place to select a gift.

BURT'S PLACE
8541 Ferris Ave, Morton Grove, 847-965-7997
No website
CUISINE: Pizza
DRINKS: Beer & Wine
SERVING: Lunch, Dinner
PRICE RANGE: $$ / CASH ONLY
NEIGHBORHOOD: Morton Grove
Great Chicago-style pizzas made with fresh ingredients with caramelized crust. Phone ahead for a reservation and pre-order for best service. Cash only.

CESAR'S RESTAURANT
3166 N Clark St, Chicago, 773-248-2835
www.killermargaritas.com
CUISINE: Mexican
DRINKS: Full Bar
SERVING: Dinner
PRICE RANGE: $$
NEIGHBORHOOD: Lakeview
This Mexican restaurant serves delicious authentic
Mexican fare and is known for its lip-smacking
margaritas. Check out their website for special events
like Cinco de Mayo and Pride Parade. Good food and
friendly service. (Try the Peach margaritas.)

THE CHICAGO CHOP HOUSE
60 W Ontario St, Chicago, 312-787-7100
www.chicagochophouse.com

CUISINE: Steakhouse
DRINKS: Full Bar
SERVING: Dinner
PRICE RANGE: $$$$
NEIGHBORHOOD: Near North Side
Located in a century-old Victorian, this place serves
Mishima Ranch Wagyu Beef and is one of the best
steakhouses in the city. Menu includes their famous
64-ounce porterhouse steak with a pretty good list of
wines by the glass. Portraits of old Chicago gangsters
(lots of those to choose from, including a few
politicians) hang on the wall and the clientele is filled
with regulars who are serious about their steaks.

THE CHICAGO DINER
3411 N Halsted St, Chicago, 773-935-6696
www.veggiediner.com
CUISINE: Vegetarian, Vegan

DRINKS: Beer & Wine Only
SERVING: Lunch, Dinner
PRICE RANGE: $$
NEIGHBORHOOD: Lakeview
A landmark vegetarian/vegan diner that has been serving good food for more than 20 years. Comfort food with a vegetarian twist. Menu favorites include: Portobello mushroom burgers and a Nacho appetizer. Yummy desserts. Even if you think you hate vegan food, give this place a try. As Lucille Ball said about Vitameatavegamin in that famous commercial, "It's so tasty, too!"

COALFIRE PIZZA
1321 W Grand Ave, Chicago, 312-226-2625
www.coalfirechicago.com
CUISINE: Pizza
DRINKS: Beer & Wine
SERVING: Lunch, Dinner
PRICE RANGE: $$
NEIGHBORHOOD: Near West Side
Here you'll find an American version of the traditional Neapolitan style pizza made in an 800-degree clean burning coal oven.

DUSEK'S
1227 W 18th St, Chicago, 312-526-3851
www.dusekschicago.com
CUISINE: American
DRINKS: Full Bar
SERVING: Dinner
PRICE RANGE: $$
NEIGHBORHOOD: Pilsen

More than a bar, this place has become a popular eatery. Menu favorites include: Boneless Duck wings, Red Snapper Crudo, and Juicy Lucy burger. A dessert favorite is the chocolate bar, served with a knife and fork as it's served on a bed of marshmallow fluff and caramel drizzle. When you leave visit the Punch Bar downstairs for one of their specialty punches.

FLORIOLE CAFÉ & BAKERY
1220 W Webster Ave, Chicago, 773-883-1313
www.floriole.com
CUISINE: Bakery/Cafe
DRINKS: No Booze
SERVING: Breakfast/Lunch
PRICE RANGE: $$
NEIGHBORHOOD: Lincoln Park
Bakery and café serving a variety of fresh pastries. Small menu of soups, salads, and quiches. Friday night is Pizza Night. Of course the coffee's great.

FRONTERA GRILL

445 N Clark St, Chicago, 312-661-1434
www.fronterakitchens.com
CUISINE: Mexican
DRINKS: Full Bar
SERVING: Lunch, Dinner
PRICE RANGE: $$$
NEIGHBORHOOD: Near North Side
Open since 1987, the popularity of this Mexican grill can probably be credited to Celebrity Chef and winner of Top Chef Masters Rick Bayless. The ever-changing menu features Mexican classics like enchiladas, mole and flautas. Menu favorites include: Oyster & Ceviche Combo and Carne Asada (Rib steak, bean and sweet plantain with a little bit of guac).

G.E.B.

841 W Randolph St, Chicago, 312-888-2258
www.gebistro.com
CUISINE: American
DRINKS: Full Bar
SERVING: Dinner
PRICE RANGE: $$$
NEIGHBORHOOD: Near West Side
This restaurant, another offering from Chef Graham Elliot, focuses on the craft of cooking with a seasonal menu. Menu favorites include: Turkey and Sage Strata and the restaurant also offers a nice selection of small production wines and craft beers. Nice selection of desserts. Great ambiance.

GIBSONS BAR & STEAKHOUSE

1028 N Rush St (bet. Cedar St & Oak St), Chicago,
312-266-8999
www.gibsonseakhouse.com
CUISINE: Steakhouse
DRINKS: Full Bar
SERVING: Lunch, Dinner
PRICE RANGE: $$$
NEIGHBORHOOD: Near North Side
This is a very popular restaurant with traditional
menu offerings of steaks, chops and seafood. The
delicious desserts are bountiful. It's busy, so book
ahead.

GILT BAR

230 W Kinzie St, Chicago, 312-464-9544
www.giltbarchicago.com
CUISINE: American
DRINKS: Full Bar

SERVING: Dinner
PRICE RANGE: $$$
NEIGHBORHOOD: Near North Side, River North
Credit the recession, but a number of good mid-price
but high-style restaurants have opened in Chicago in
the last two years. A favorite is "Gilt Bar," a casual
restaurant in the River North neighborhood that isn't
casual about its cooking. The menu features New
American dishes like blackened cauliflower with
capers ($7) and ricotta gnocchi with sage and brown
butter ($13). After dinner, head downstairs to Curio, a
basement bar with a Prohibition theme. Try the
Death's Door Daisy, made with artisanal Wisconsin
vodka and Aperol, a blood orange liqueur, for $10.

GIRL & THE GOAT
809 W Randolph St (bct. Green & Halsted Sts),
Chicago, 312-492-6262
www.girlandthegoat.com
CUISINE: American
DRINKS: Full Bar
SERVING: Dinner
PRICE RANGE: $$$
NEIGHBORHOOD: Near West Side, West Loop
A much-blogged-about new restaurant where the
"Top Chef" winner Stephanie Izard takes livestock
parts seriously. The often-updated menu recently
included lamb ribs with grilled avocado and pistachio
piccata, and braised beef tongue with masa and beef
vinaigrette. If you're not a carnivore, try chickpeas

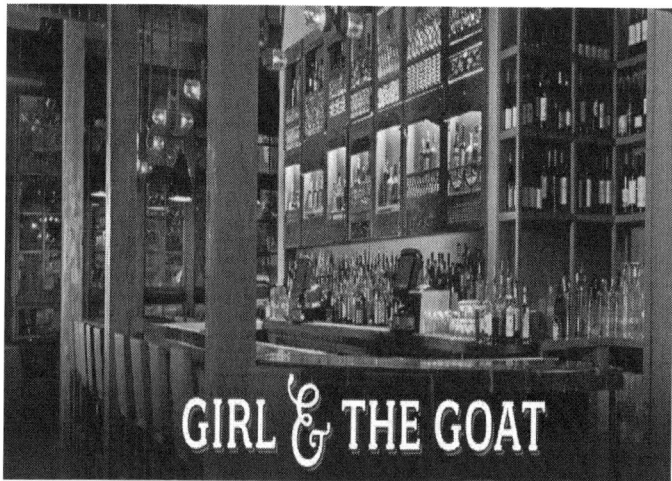

GIRL & THE GOAT

three ways, and for dessert, potato fritters with lemon poached eggplant and Greek yogurt. The soaring dining room, designed by the Chicago design firm 555 International, is warm and modern, with exposed beams, walls of charred cedar and a large open kitchen.

GREEN ZEBRA
1460 W Chicago Ave, Chicago, 312-243-7100
www.greenzebrachicago.com
CUISINE: Vegetarian
DRINKS: Full Bar
SERVING: Dinner
PRICE RANGE: $$$
NEIGHBORHOOD: Noble Square
A vegetarian's delight. Also vegan dishes. Menu items include: Chickpea Salad and Housemade Coconut Curry. Nice wine selection. Tasty desserts too.

HENRI
18 S Michigan Ave, Chicago, 312-578-0763
www.henrichicago.com
CUISINE: French/American
DRINKS: Full Bar
SERVING: Dinner
PRICE RANGE: $$$$
NEIGHBORHOOD: The Loop
Henri serves traditional French cuisine with menu favorites like Diver Scallops with Pimente d'espelette and Peekytoe Crab with a potato custard. Nice tasting menu and delicious desserts like creme brûlée and dark chocolate ganache. Carefully curated wine list and creative cocktails. Upscale dining experience.

HONKY TONK BARBEQUE
800 S Racine Ave, Chicago, 312-226-7427

www.honkytonkbbqchicago.com
CUISINE: Barbeque
DRINKS: Full Bar
SERVING: Dinner
PRICE RANGE: $$
NEIGHBORHOOD: Pilsen
Popular hangout offering a full schedule of live music
that covers the genres of American Roots music
including: roaring 20s, groovy 60s; Western Swing,
Honky Tonk, Rockabilly, Bluegrass, Blues, Old
Time, Soul, and occasionally new age indie and rock.
Menu features Championship BBQ pork, beef,
chicken and other made-from-scratch dishes. This is a
late night bar with theme nights like Trivia night on
Wednesdays.

JAM
3057 W Logan Blvd, Chicago, 773-292-6011
www.jamrestaurant.com
CUISINE: Breakfast, Brunch
DRINKS: Full Bar
SERVING: Breakfast, Brunch
PRICE RANGE: $$
NEIGHBORHOOD: Logan Square
While this restaurant serves both breakfast and lunch,
it has earned a reputation as one of the nation's most
celebrated brunch restaurants. Chef Jeffrey Mauro
offers a creative menu featuring favorites like: the egg
sandwich, the burrito suizo, and malted French toast.

JELLYFISH
1009 N Rush St #2, Chicago, 312-660-3111
www.jellyfishchicago.com

CUISINE: Sushi, Asian Fusion
DRINKS: Full Bar
SERVING: Lunch, Dinner
PRICE RANGE: $$$
NEIGHBORHOOD: Near North Side
An intimate pan-Asian restaurant and lounge offering a special dining experience. This 95-seat restaurant, located on the second floor about the trendy boutiques of Rush Street, features a personalized menu that is sure to please. Menu favorites include Chicken lettuce wraps and Touched Salmon roll.

KITCHEN SINK CAFÉ
1107 W Berwyn Ave, Chicago, 773-944-0592
www.kitchensinkcafe.blogspot.com
CUISINE: American
DRINKS: No Boozc
SERVING: Breakfast, Lunch
PRICE RANGE: $
NEIGHBORHOOD: Near West Side
A comfortable neighborhood coffee shop offering a typical American menu of breakfast sandwiches, hot lunches, and favorites like mac n' cheese.

LITTLE GOAT BREAD
820 W Randolph St, Chicago, 312 888 3455
www.littlegoatchicago.com
CUISINE: American/Bakery
DRINKS: Full Bar
SERVING: Breakfast, Lunch, Dinner
PRICE RANGE: $$
NEIGHBORHOOD: Near West Side

Celebrated Chef Stephanie Izard offers a simple menu of American favorites in this updated version of a diner with things like Shrimp & Grits and Bull's Eye French Toast. Comfortable diner-like atmosphere.

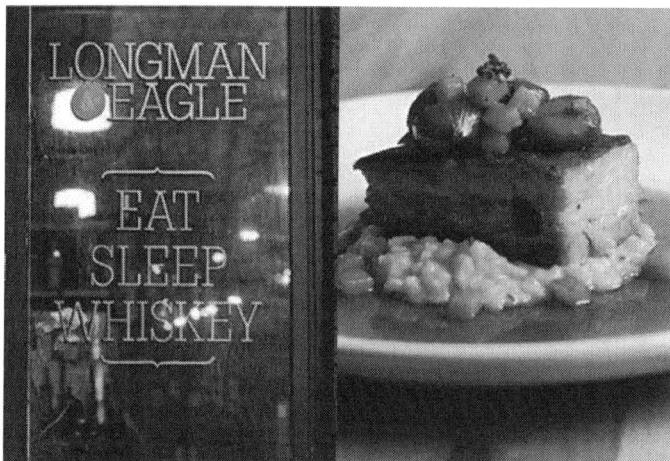

Photo credits: Imaginary Frend, Longman & Eagle website

LONGMAN & EAGLE
2657 N Kedzie Ave, (bet. Milwaukee & Schubert Aves), Chicago, 773-276-7110
www.longmanandeagle.com
CUISINE: American
DRINKS: Full Bar
SERVING: Breakfast, Lunch & Dinner
PRICE RANGE: $$
NEIGHBORHOOD: Logan Square
It is a rough-edged bar that serves a refined brunch: a chunky sockeye salmon tartare with pickled mango ($10) or a wild boar "Sloppy Joe" ($10). Six hotel rooms upstairs. Logan Square, about five to six miles northwest of the Loop, is a remnant of Chicago's late-

19th-century beautification movement, with a statue of an eagle by Evelyn Longman where two of the grandest boulevards meet.

MAUDE'S LIQUOR BAR
840 W Randolph St, Chicago, 312-243-9712
www.maudesliquorbar.com
CUISINE: French
DRINKS: Full Bar
SERVING: Dinner
PRICE RANGE: $$$
NEIGHBORHOOD: Near West Side
Run by **Au Cheval** owner Brendan Sodikoff, Maude's is certainly more than a liquor bar. On the first floor there's a dining room with a marble bar and on the second there's a sunken, plush bar. Menu favorites include: Steak tartare, Mussels, and French Onion fondue. Nice wine list. Romantic atmosphere.

MIA FRANCESCA

3311 N Clark St, Chicago, 773-281-3310
www.miafrancesca.com
CUISINE: Italian
DRINKS: Full Bar
SERVING: Dinner
PRICE RANGE: $$
NEIGHBORHOOD: Lakeview
Popular chain restaurant in these parts serving solid if
not terribly imaginative Italian fare. Noisy and
crowded. Menu favorites include: Rigatoni con
scarola and chicken salvia. Outdoor patio.

MOTT ST

1401 N Ashland Ave, Chicago, 773-687-9977
www.mottstreetchicago.com
CUISINE: Asian Fusion
DRINKS: Full Bar
SERVING: Dinner
PRICE RANGE: $$
NEIGHBORHOOD: Wicker Park
A lovely restaurant with an Asian street food-inspired
menu. Menu favorites include: Whiskey-marinated
pork neck, Crab Brain fried rice, and Oyster
Mushrooms. Desserts include a Choco Banana,
Mantou (yeasted doughnuts in chocolate) and Tres
Leches Cake. A great dining experience especially if
you share multiple plates.

NELLICOTE
833 W Randolph St, Chicago, 312-432-0500
www.nellcoterestaurant.com
CUISINE: French, Italian
DRINKS: Full Bar
SERVING: Brunch, Dinner
PRICE RANGE: $$$
NEIGHBORHOOD: Near West Side
This high-energy nightspot offers an eclectic décor
with Art Nouveau wrought-iron gates, Italian marble
grand staircase, crystal chandeliers and Grand
Dosssier Toliix bar chairs. Here you'll find kitchen-
crafted cocktails and European-inspired tapas made
with Midwestern ingredients. Menu favorites include
the pizzas and pastas made from house-milled
Midwestern wheat.

NIGHTWOOD

2119 S Halsted St (at 21st Place), Chicago, 312-526-3385

www.nightwoodrestaurant.com

CUISINE: American

DRINKS: Full Bar

SERVING: Dinner

PRICE RANGE: $$$

NEIGHBORHOOD: Pilsen

It is off the beaten path with its Pilsen location, comfortable laid-back decor, and great pure simple food. Menu is handwritten daily, so things change as they bring in food and produce from their handpicked suppliers, but when we were there, we tried: crispy pig ears with homemade butter; fried squid, braised rabbit in savory cabbage, wood-grilled Wisconsin trout, fluke from Maine, thick-cut bacon on polenta. Excellent.

NOMI

Park Hyatt Chicago, 800 N Michigan Ave, Chicago,
312-239-4030
www.hyatt.com/gallery/nomi
CUISINE: American
DRINKS: Full Bar
SERVING: Breakfast, Lunch, Dinner
PRICE RANGE: $$$$
NEIGHBORHOOD: Near North Side
Located on the seventh floor of the Park Hyatt
Chicago, this elegant restaurant offers a simple menu
featuring flavorful dishes made from regionally-
sourced ingredients. Menu favorites include: Seafood
salad, Pork belly with escargot and Pork secreto. Nice
wine and beer list and cocktail menu.

NORTH POND RESTAURANT

2610 N Cannon Dr, Chicago, 773-477-5845
www.northpondrestaurant.com
CUISINE: American
DRINKS: Full Bar
SERVING: Dinner
PRICE RANGE: $$$$
NEIGHBORHOOD: Lincoln Park
Located within the grounds of Lincoln Park, North
Pond boasts one of the loveliest settings in the city.
Set in a structure built in 1912 that was originally a
warming shelter for ice skaters, Chef Bruce Sherman
offers a creative seasonal menu of "upscale" New
American cuisine. Menu favorites include: Grilled
smoke sturgeon and Grass Fed Beef. Great tasting

menu. Dessert choices include: chocolate mousse and cranberry sorbet.

PARSON'S CHICKEN & FISH
2952 W Armitage St, Chicago, 773-384-3333
www.parsonschickenandfish.com
CUISINE: American
DRINKS: Full Bar
SERVING: Lunch & Dinner
PRICE RANGE: $
NEIGHBORHOOD: Logan Square
Absolutely nothing fancy about this popular take-out spot selling fried chicken and fish. You can sit inside or outside. The grilled chicken is cooked Amish style (with citrus, scallions, rum, Habanero and spices), and you can get 2 pieces, a half chicken or a whole one. The fish fry comes with 3 piece, 6 pieces, or 9. The fish sandwich, however, is better, and comes

with beer-battered fish, cole slaw and American cheese. (Get a side order of hush puppies.)

PARTHENON
314 S Halsted St, Chicago, 312-726-2407
www.theparthenon.com
CUISINE: Greek
DRINKS: Full Bar
SERVING: Lunch, Dinner
PRICE RANGE: $$
NEIGHBORHOOD: Greektown
A local family oriented restaurant serving authentic Greek cuisine. Menu favorites include: Saganaki (flaming cheese), Taramasalata (fish roe dip), Moussaka (beef and eggplant casserole), and Pastichio (a Greek lasagna with noodles and beef). Free valet parking.

PENNY'S NOODLE SHOP
3400 N Sheffield Ave, Chicago, 773-281-8222
www.pennysnoodleshop.com
CUISINE: Thai
DRINKS: Beer & Wine only
SERVING: Lunch, Dinner
PRICE RANGE: $
NEIGHBORHOOD: Lakeview
Cheap but tasty Thai & Asian cuisine. Menu favorites include: Hot Peppered Noodles and Sautéed Chicken.

PIZZERIA DE NELLA
1443 W Fullerton Ave, Chicago, 773-281-6600
www.pizzeriadanella.com
CUISINE: Pizza

DRINKS: Full Bar
SERVING: Lunch, Dinner
PRICE RANGE: $$
NEIGHBORHOOD: Lincoln Park, DePaul
This neighborhood pizza eatery offers a variety of pizzas, pasta, salad, wings, and subs. Daily specials. Dine in or delivery.

THE PUBLICAN
837 W Fulton Market St, Chicago, 312-733-9555
www.thepublicanrestaurant.com
CUISINE: American
DRINKS: Full Bar
SERVING: Lunch (but late, opens at 3:30) & dinner nightly; weekend brunch from 10
PRICE RANGE: $$$
NEIGHBORHOOD: Fulton Market, Near West Side, West Loop

Known in these parts for their oysters, carefully selected pork, and beer. The menu is very much seasonal. Expect items like wild king salmon roe, smoked arctic char, duck hearts (with kale marmalade), blood sausages, sucking pig, porchetta. There's even a daily pickle selection. They have a sticky bun bread pudding for dessert that's different and pleasing.

PUMP ROOM
1301 N State Pkwy, Chicago, 312-229-6740
www.pumproom.com
CUISINE: American
DRINKS: Full Bar
SERVING: Breakfast, Lunch, Dinner
PRICE RANGE: $$$
NEIGHBORHOOD: Near North Side
Fans of the old Pump Room (the few who are alive) will delight at the changes brought on by world-renowned chef Jean-Georges Vongerichten who has

reinvented the classics from the old menu. J-G is in his best "farm to table" experience here in the Pump Room offering regional specialties. Menu offerings include a variety of late-night tapas style small plates. The bar offers specialty cocktails and a beer menu including draft and bottles. Chef Kady Yon offers a creative selection of desserts including a cheese cake made with homemade grape sorbet and figs and a deep dish cookie with a molten chocolate center.

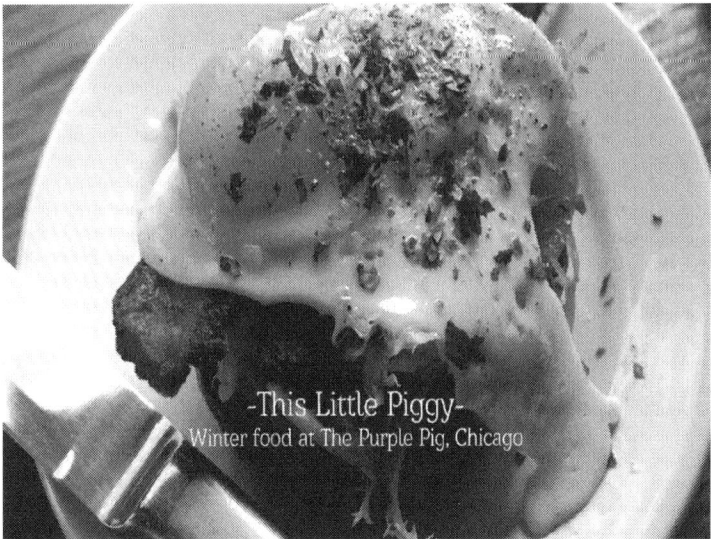

-This Little Piggy-
Winter food at The Purple Pig, Chicago

THE PURPLE PIG
500 N Michigan Ave, Chicago, 312-464-1744
www.purplepigchicago.com
CUISINE: Tapas/Mediterrannean
DRINKS: Full Bar
SERVING: Lunch, Dinner
PRICE RANGE: $$
NEIGHBORHOOD: Near North Side

This is an intimate gastropub run by Jimmy Bannos Jr offering a tasting adventure for foodies. Here you'll find dishes you won't find anywhere else. Menu favorites include: Milk braised pork shoulder and Pork neck bone gravy with ricotta. There's also a great wine list and impressive offering of beers. Usually a long wait for tables. No reservations.

RUSSIAN TEA TIME
77 E Adams St, Chicago, 312-360-0000
www.russianteatime.com
CUISINE: Russian
DRINKS: Full Bar
SERVING: Lunch, Dinner
PRICE RANGE: $$$
NEIGHBORHOOD: The Loop
One visit to this landmark Russian restaurant and you'll feel like part of the family. (Well, it might take two visits.) Typical Russian fare like Beef Stroganoff, Chicken Roulette, Ukrainian borscht, herring. Other regional cuisines represented are Uzbek, Azerbaijani and Moldavian. The Tea Service itself offers over 30 different teas, but that's not as important as the unusual pastries, sweets and other savories you get to choose from, including rugelach and Pozharski croquettes. Don't overlook the "vodka flights" that include various flavored vodkas. The wine selection, as you can imagine in a place like this, is wide ranging and carries labels you've never heard of.

SCHWA
1466 N Ashland Ave, Chicago, 773-252-1466
www.schwarestaurant.com

CUISINE: American
DRINKS: No Booze
SERVING: Dinner
PRICE RANGE: $$$$
NEIGHBORHOOD: Wicker Park
Here fine cuisine becomes a dining experience. Chef
Michael Carlson serves up a menu of vivid courses
featuring seasonal ingredients from around the world.
A nine-course meal here is an unforgettable
experience. Check out the tasting menu.

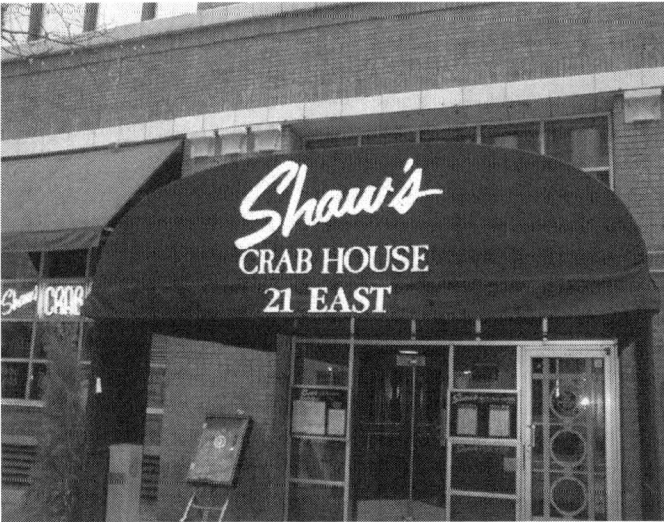

SHAW'S CRAB HOUSE
21 E Hubbard St, Chicago, 312-527-2722
www.shawscrabhouse.com
CUISINE: Seafood, Sushi Bar
DRINKS: Full Bar
SERVING: Lunch, Dinner
PRICE RANGE: $$$

NEIGHBORHOOD: Near North Side
Shaw's is actually two restaurants in one – a
sophisticated seafood restaurant and an energetic
oyster bar. Both offer a menu featuring top-grade fish
and shellfish, oysters, and sushi and sashimi
combinations. Menu favorites include the Maryland
crab cake and the oysters (East and West Coast
varieties). Bustling happy hour.

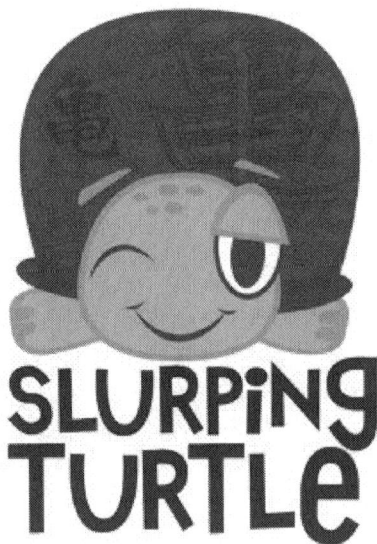

THE SLURPING TURTLE
116 W Hubbard St, Chicago, 312-464-0466
www.slurpingturtle.com
CUISINE: Japanese
DRINKS: Full Bar
SERVING: Lunch, Dinner
PRICE RANGE: $$
NEIGHBORHOOD: Near North Side

Here Chef Takashi hopes to recreate his childhood culinary experiences in Japan with his version of Japanese Comfort food. Menu favorites include: Saikyo Eggplant, Pork Belly Snack, and Duck Fat Fried Chicken. Lounge area downstairs with bottle service.

THE SMOKE DADDY
1804 W Division St, Chicago, 773-772-6656
www.thesmokedaddy.com
CUISINE: Barbeque
DRINKS: Full Bar
SERVING: Lunch, Dinner
PRICE RANGE: $$
NEIGHBORHOOD: Wicker Park
Barbecue sandwiches, down-home specials, and really loud music. Old time barbeque joint that serves barbeque chicken and pork, down-home specials, ribs, mac 'n cheese and even has a veggie burger. Interesting cocktails like the Bloody Mary garnished with meat. Live music. Known for its world famous Chicago BBQ sauce.

SOLA
3868 N Lincoln Ave, Chicago, 773-327-3868
www.sola-restaurant.com
CUISINE: American, Hawaiian, Asian Fusion
DRINKS: Full Bar
SERVING: Dinner nightly from 5:30; weekend brunch from 10 – 2
PRICE RANGE: $$$
NEIGHBORHOOD: North Center

Sola's cuisine is inspired by the traditions of many cultures as perfected in Hawaiian kitchens. Menu favorites include: Artichoke fritters with truffle aioli; Kalua pork with banana bread; gnocchi but with a twist, sweet potato dumplings. Busy during weekend brunch. Outdoor seating.

SOUTHPORT GROCERY & CAFÉ
3552 N Southport Ave, (betw. Addison St & Eddy St), Chicago, 773-665-0100
www.southportgrocery.com
CUISINE: American
DRINKS: Full bar
SERVING: Breakfast & Lunch (sometimes does dinner, but usually only Thursday and Friday—check to be sure)
PRICE RANGE: $$
NEIGHBORHOOD: Lakeview

A pioneer of the restaurant-plus-market concept, the chef and owner, Lisa Santos, still does it right. The airy, bright dining room has booth tables along the side wall and the staff's market picks on the blackboard: pork belly with Fat Toad Farm goat milk caramel sauce from Vermont, feta from nearby Prairie Pure Farm. The eclectic menu is strong in grown-up kids' fare -- cupcake pancakes, stuffed French toast, grilled Brie sandwiches, artisanal Italian sodas -- and starred items are available in the grocery. Ms. Santos's kitchen also makes and packages a line of products for the market, including bread pudding pancake mix, granola and blueberry preserves.

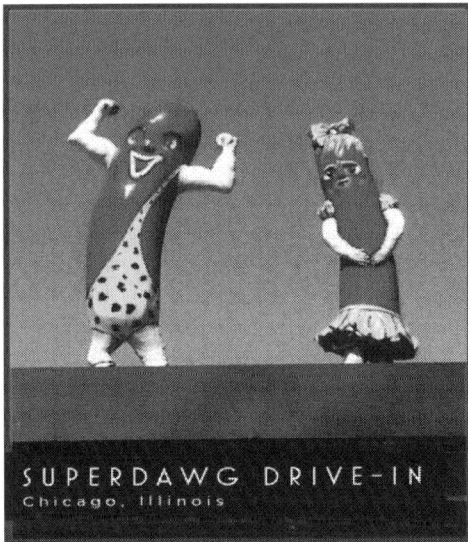

SUPERDAWG DRIVE-IN
Chicago, Illinois

SUPERDAWG DRIVE-IN
6363 N Milwaukee Ave, Chicago, 773-763-0660
www.superdawg.com
CUISINE: Hot dogs, Hamburgers

DRINKS: No Booze
SERVING: Lunch & Dinner
PRICE RANGE: $
NEIGHBORHOOD: Norwood Park
This is an iconic hot dog drive-in. Really fun to come here. They make their own hot dogs and serve piping hot fries that are out of this world. Everything on the menu is tasty but not if you're counting calories. The malts are the best. This is a drive-in. Limited indoor standing space. There are picnic tables when the weather is nice.

TAC QUICK THAI KITCHEN
3930 N Sheridan Rd, Chicago, 773-327-5253
www.tacquick.net
CUISINE: Thai
DRINKS: No Booze
SERVING: Lunch & Dinner
PRICE RANGE: $$
NEIGHBORHOOD: Wrigleyville
This top-notch Thai eatery features a creative menu with dishes like cookie-cutter curries and pad thais. Ask for the second menu where you'll discover items like the tart and smoky pork and rice sausage and ground chicken with crispy basil and preserved eggs. Check out the specials.

TANGO SUR
3763 N Southport Ave, Chicago, 773-477-5466
www.tangosur.net
CUISINE: Steakhouse; Argentine
DRINKS: No Booze; BYOB (no corkage fee)
SERVING: Dinner

PRICE RANGE: $$
NEIGHBORHOOD: Lakeview
This family-style Argentinean steakhouse, with two
dining areas, serves delicious steaks. Large portions.
They have no alcohol but have a no corkage BYOB
policy. Menu favorites include: Empanadas and
Melted provolone served with red peppers; sliced
eggplant served in vinegar; breaded beef Milanesa
with 2 fried eggs on top; churrasco steaks, grilled half
chicken; grilled short ribs served with sausages. Very
busy and there's usually a wait.

TAVERNITA
151 W Erie St, Chicago, 312-274-1111
www.tavernita.com
CUISINE: Tapas/Mediterrannean/American (New)
DRINKS: Full Bar
SERVING: Dinner

PRICE RANGE: $$$
NEIGHBORHOOD: Near North Side
This popular eatery offers an interesting mix of
American dishes with influences from France, Italy
and Spain. The small plate menu encourages
sampling and sharing with menu favorites like: Pork
belly sliders, Corn pudding, Halibut with avocado and
Balsamic Glazed mushrooms.

TERZO PIANO
159 E Monroe St, Chicago, 312-443-8650
www.terzopianochicago.com
CUISINE: Italian
DRINKS: Full Bar
SERVING: Lunch
PRICE RANGE: $$$
NEIGHBORHOOD: The Loop
Located in the new Modern Wing of the Art Institute
of Chicago, this is a great place for lunch or Sunday

Brunch. Chef Tony Mantuano, known for his four-star Italian restaurant Spiaggia, uses fresh, organic, and sustainably produced ingredients for his seasonal menus. Menu favorites include: Margherita pizza and Sausage flatbread. Nice wine list.

TRENCHERMAN
2039 W North Ave, Chicago, 773-661-1540
www.trenchermen.com
CUISINE: American, Modern European
DRINKS: Full Bar
SERVING: Dinner
PRICE RANGE: $$$
NEIGHBORHOOD: Wicker Park
Billed as "a restaurant and bar built for the everyman," this place offers a Midwestern farm-focused twist to new American cuisine. The setting is casual but it has the feel of fine dining in the 86-seat

dining room. Menu favorites include: Kale salad with fried egg, Whitefish with greens and bacon, and Artic char served with brussels sprouts, lentils and sage pesto. Creative cocktails. Beautiful space.

URBAN BELLY
3053 N California Ave, Chicago, 773-583-0500
www.urbanbellychicago.com
www.cornerstonerestaurants.com/urban-belly
CUISINE: Asian Fusion, noddle Shop, Vietnamese
DRINKS: No Booze; BYOB, no corkage fee
SERVING: Lunch & Dinner
PRICE RANGE: $$
NEIGHBORHOOD: Avondale
The unprepossessing brick building in which you find Bill Kim's operation is deceptively modest. Just a couple of long common tables you share with others, but the food is perfect: mushroom pho; pad Thai; kimchi stew with pork belly, noodles, broth; Wagyu

pot stickers; stir fry brisket; Soba noodle soup with bay scallops, oyster mushrooms and Thai basil broth. The pork and cilantro dumplings are tasty.

VERA
1023 W Lake St, Chicago, 312-243-9770
www.**verachicago**.com
CUISINE: Spanish/Tapas
DRINKS: Full Bar
SERVING: Dinner
PRICE RANGE: $$$
NEIGHBORHOOD: Near West Side
This is an intimate wine bar with an impressive selection of seasonal wines from Spain, Europe and

the Americas. Menu consists of Spanish small plates so sharing is encouraged. Menu favorites include: Octopus, Kale, Manchego salad, and Fried chickpeas. Reservations recommended. Creative desserts like salted caramel pudding.

XOCO
449 N Clark St, Chicago, 312-334-3688
www.rickbayless.com
CUISINE: Mexican
DRINKS: Beer & Wine Only
SERVING: Lunch & Dinner; closed Sunday and Monday
PRICE RANGE: $$
NEIGHBORHOOD: Near North Side
Rick Bayless has a mini restaurant empire here in Chicago, and this is one of his stars. It's not fast food Mexican, but rapid enough to be confused as fast food. No question that it's good: churros fresh from the fryer. Empanada, Mexican hot chocolate (they grind the Mexican cacao beans in the front window), tortas (Mexican sub sandwiches), caldos (meal-in-a-bowl soups with veggies, seafood or pork belly). Only seats 40 and they don't take reservations, so plan on going early or late.

YUSHO

2853 N Kedzie Ave, (bet. Diversey Pky & Georges
St), Chicago, 773-904-8558
www.yusho-chicago.com
CUISINE: Japanese
DRINKS: Full Bar
SERVING: Dinner nightly except Tuesday when it's
closed; Sunday, opens at noon
PRICE RANGE: $$$
NEIGHBORHOOD: Avondale
Matthias Merges was the Chef de Cuisine at Charlie
Trotter's for 15 years. Trotter closed its doors in
2012. This charming small yakatori-style restaurant
was designed by Merges' wife. Traditional specialties
like bok choy, tuna tataki, octopus, tempura, squid.
Painstakingly prepared.

NIGHTLIFE

ALLIUM RESTAURANT AND BAR CHICAGO
Four Seasons Hotel
120 E Delaware Pl, Chicago, 312-799-4900
www.alliumchicago.com
CUISINE: American
DRINKS: Full Bar
SERVING: Breakfast, Lunch, Dinner
PRICE RANGE: $$$
NEIGHBORHOOD: Near North Side

This is one of those classy hotel bars serving creative cocktails. If you get hungry there is a snack menu that includes tasty treats like: Mushrooms n' Toast, Crispy Brussels Sprouts and Roasted Carrots.

THE AVIARY
955 W Fulton Market St, Chicago, 312-226-0868
www.theaviary.com
NEIGHBORHOOD: Fulton Market, Near West Side, West Loop
If you think you can just saunter up to the bar at the Aviary, think again. A limited number of reservations are accepted each day for seatings at 6, 8 and 10 p.m. Would-be patrons must e-mail their requests to reservations@theaviary.com. If selected, you will be contacted by 4 p.m. the day of the reservation. So much for advance planning. Owned by Chef Grant Achatz and his partner, Nick Kokonas, owners of celebrated Chicago restaurants like Alinea, this bar offers specialty cocktails that you won't find anywhere else, like the Tropic Thunder served in a specially designed glass called the porthole. Another specialty cocktail called the Ford's Model Tea Party is made with Ford's gin, Old Pulteney Scotch and Atsby Armadillo Cake vermouth, Mandarine Napoleon and Sicilian blood orange tea and is served in a china cup. Great list of beers from small brewers. A must-see for cocktail lovers.

THE BARRELHOUSE FLAT
2624 N Lincoln Ave, Chicago, 773-857-0421
www.barrelhouseflat.com
NEIGHBORHOOD: Lincoln Park

Two-level cocktail lounge – first floor offers a casual atmosphere with the upstairs being a bit more intimate (and there's often a waiting list). The place is a bit trendy serving craft cocktails but there's an impressive beer and wine list. Menu of small plate snacks available. Charming interior with velour seating.

BERNARD'S
Waldorf-Astoria
11 East Walton St, Chicago, 312-646-1300
www.waldorfastoriachicagohotel.com
NEIGHBORHOOD: Gold Coast
Hidden in a corner on the second floor of the Waldorf-Astoria hotel, this attractive bar serves delicious specialty cocktails from an ever-changing menu. This bar makes its own bitters and syrups with a beer list featuring small brewers. Great atmosphere

with music selections featuring performers like Billie
Holiday and Ella Fitzgerald.

BIG CHICKS
5024 N Sheridan Rd, (bet. Argyle St & Carmen Ave),
Chicago, 773-728-5511
www.bigchicks.com
NEIGHBORHOOD: Uptown
There are so many clubs on Ontario Street, just north
of the Loop, that it's sometimes known as Red Bull
Row. To ease out of a troubled day, go to Big Chicks,
a gay bar that welcomes everyone. The drinks are

cheap, the crowd is friendly and the décor is nicely weird.

BILLY SUNDAY
3143 West Logan Blvd, Chicago, 773-661-2485
www.billy-sunday.com
NEIGHBORHOOD: Logan Square
A dark and charming craft-cocktail joint that serves creative cocktails befitting a chemist. There's also a delightful menu of dishes prepared by Chef John Vermiglio.

BLUE FROG BAR & GRILL
676 N La Salle St, Chicago, 312-943-8900
www.bluefrogbarandgrill.com
NEIGHBORHOOD: Near North Side

This is one of the most popular karaoke bars in Chicago. The crowd is supportive and it's a fun hangout.

BUDDY GUY'S LEGENDS
700 S. Wabash, Chicago, 312-427-1190
www.buddyguy.com
NEIGHBORHOOD: South Loop
Known as the nation's premier blues club, this club offers an impressive roster of local, national, and international blues acts. Some of the talents that have performed here include: Van Morrison, Willie Dixon, The Rolling Stones, Lou Rawls, David Bowie, John Mayer, Stevie Ray Vaughan, and The Pointer Sisters. Buddy Guy takes the stage every January with a series of sold out shows. Open 7 nights a week. Southern Cajun soul food menu available. Check website for schedule and prices.

CALIFORNIA CLIPPER BAR
1002 N California Ave, Chicago, 773-384-2547
www.californiaclipper.com
NEIGHBORHOOD: Humboldt Park
This is a restored cocktail lounge that's out of another era. Here you'll find board games instead of TVs. Chicago's only bar with grape soda in the gun. Live music Fridays and Saturdays. Monday night is Trivia Night. Cash only.

CAROL'S PUB
4659 N Clark St, Chicago, 773-334-2402
www.carolspubchicago.com
NEIGHBORHOOD: Uptown

This is one of those redneck Honky Tonk country bars that's been around over three decades. Bar holds about 250. God help me, but it's open at 9 a.m. on Monday and Tuesday, 11 a.m. the rest of the week. Live country bands. Cover charge.

CHARLIE'S CHICAGO
3726 N Broadway St, Chicago, 773-871-8887
www.charlieschicago.com
NEIGHBORHOOD: Lakeview
Gay country themed dance club with the best in entertainment, 7 days a week. Charlie's Chicago offers a roster that includes: award-winning country programming, after-hours dance party, Bingo, Karaoke, and free dance lessons. Resident & Guest DJs and light shows. Open until 4 a.m. Cover charge.

THE CLOSET
3325 N Broadway St, Chicago, 773-477-8533
www.theclosetchicago.com
NEIGHBORHOOD: Lakeview
Open since 1978, this neighborhood bar, although known as a lesbian bar, welcomes everyone. A friendly joint with games like darts and video bowling. Free Wi-Fi. TVs feature sports and music videos. Karaoke on Thursday nights. Theme parties.

THE COMEDY BAR
157 W Ontario St, Chicago, 773-387-8412
www.comedybarchicago.com
NEIGHBORHOOD: Near North Side, River North
It offers performances on Fridays and Saturdays at 8 and 10 p.m. You won't find big names, but a hit-or-miss roster of itinerant comedians, some who heckle the audience in language that can't be printed here.

$10 cover includes admission to the upstairs lounge, where bottle-service vodkas start at $200.

↓

THE DRAWING ROOM
937 North Rush St, Chicago, 312-266-2694
www.thedrchicago.com
NEIGHBORHOOD: Near North Side
A subterranean cocktail lounge that serves creative cocktails with a menu featuring quality late-night fare. Here you'll find fine food and cocktails in an intimate setting.

DRUMBAR at RAFFAELLO HOTEL
201 E Delaware Pl, Chicago, 312-924-2531
www.drumbar.com
NEIGHBORHOOD: Near North Side
Located on top of the Raffaello Hotel, this popular rooftop bar offers a menu of creative cocktails.

There's an intimate indoor lounge and an outdoor terrace that offers beautiful views of Lake Michigan.

ELIXIR

3452 N Halsted, (bet. Newport Ave & Cornelia Ave), Chicago, 773-975-9244
www.elixirchicago.com
NEIGHBORHOOD: Lakeview
In Boystown, where you can easily find a place to sing show tunes, dance or screen "RuPaul's Drag Race," Elixir is a nice spot to relax. Specialty cocktails are big here.

EMPTY BOTTLE

1035 N Western Ave, Chicago, 773-276-3600
www.emptybottle.com
NEIGHBORHOOD: Ukrainian Village
This popular live music venue offers a schedule of local and independent music. Cash only. Menu features some great local breweries. It's a bit divey but friendly.

HAYMARKET PUB & BREWERY

737 W Randolph St, Chicago, 312-638-0700
www.haymarketbrewing.com
NEIGHBORHOOD: Near West Side
This pub features two separate areas – one for the bar and the other for dining. Guests can actually see the fermentation room where the beer is made. This place attracts an interesting crowd as it's the home of Chicago's Drinking & Writing Theater. Great beer selection with over 30 on tap. Appetizer menu available.

THE HIDEOUT
1354 W Wabansia Ave, Chicago, 773-227-4433
www.hideoutchicago.com
NEIGHBORHOOD: Noble Square
Open since 1934, this small music venue that looks like a dive bar is very prominent in Chicago's live music scene and offers a schedule of live music, theatrical performances, dance parties and comedy shows. Billed as "a regular guy bar for irregular folks who just don't fit in." Artists who have played here include Neko Case, Wilco and Mavis Staples. Check website for schedule.

HOUSE OF BLUES
329 N Dearborn St, Chicago, 312-923-2000
www.houseofblues.com/chicago
NEIGHBORHOOD: Near North Side
Whether you want a gospel brunch or a late-night jam fest, it's worth checking the schedule at House of

Blues Chicago, which has featured artists like the Who and Al Green. Popular music venue with locations all over the U.S. This venue attracts big-name performers from all genres including jazz, blues, gospel, alternative rock and hop-hop. Interior is a mix of blues bar and opera house. There's a second-stage in the restaurant offering live blues nightly. Check out the popular Sunday gospel brunch.

HYDRATE
3458 N Halsted St, Chicago, 773-975-9244
www.hydratechicago.com
NEIGHBORHOOD: Lakeview
Known as Chicago's Premier Gay Dance Club, offers a fun night featuring theme nights, drag shows and dancers. Cover Charge. Open 7 nights.

JAZZ SHOWCASE
806 S Plymouth Ct, Chicago, 312-360-0234
www.jazzshowcase.com
NEIGHBORHOOD: South Loop
Founded in 1947 by Joe Segal, this is the oldest jazz club in Chicago. The 170 seat venue offers a roster of some of the best jazz acts in Chicago. Some of the greats who have performed here include: Chris Potter, Frank Morgan, James Carter, Stu Katz, McCoy Tyner, Dexter Gordon, Richie Cole, Dizzy Gillespie, George Benson, and Joe Farrell. Check website for schedule and prices. Cover charge.

MURPHY'S BLEACHERS
3655 N Sheffield St (between Addison St & Waveland Ave), Chicago, 773-281-5356

www.murphysbleachers.com
NEIGHBORHOOD: Wrigleyville, Lakeview
Founded in the 1930s as Ernie's Bleachers, a hot dog
stand hawking beer by the pail, Murphy's Bleachers is
now a perpetually packed sports bar across the street
from -- what else? -- the bleachers at Wrigley Field.
Never mind that the Cubs haven't won a World Series
since 1908. You can enjoy beers with the throngs who
love them anyway.

ROOF ON THE WIT
201 N State St, Chicago, 312-239-9502
www.thewithotel.com
NEIGHBORHOOD: The Loop
Upscale rooftop lounge located on the 27th floor of
the Wit Hotel. Great summer scene. Creative
cocktails and snack menu. Great spot for a first date
when the weather permits.

ROSA'S LOUNGE
3420 W Armitage Ave, Chicago, 773-342-0452
www.rosaslounge.com
NEIGHBORHOOD: Logan Square
A family-owned blues lounge that features a variety
of styles showcasing legendary singers like David
Honeyboy Edwards, Homesick James and Pinetop.

ROSCOE'S
3356 N Halsted St, Chicago, 773-281-3355
www.roscoes.com
NEIGHBORHOOD: Lakeview
Since 1987, Roscoe's has been entertaining crowds.
By day, it's a neighborhood bar with a sidewalk café
but by night Roscoe's transforms into a lively
nightclub with a great dance floor. Theme nights,
drag shows, boy dancers, and Karaoke on Mondays &
Wednesdays. Cover charge.

SCOFFLAW
3201 W Armitage Ave, Chicago, 773-252-9700
www.scofflawchicago.com
NEIGHBORHOOD: Logan Square
A popular neighborhood bar that serves great
cocktails like Sly Devil made with Scofflaw Old Tom
gin. The food is good too, particularly the burgers.
There are tables but they're hard to come by and
there's always a wait.

SIMON'S
5210 N Clark St, Chicago, 773-878-0894
www.simonstavern.com
NEIGHBORHOOD: Andersonville/Uptown
One of Chicago's old time favorite dive bars. Ok beer
selection on tap and good Glogg. Juke box for music.
Cash only.

SIDETRACK
3349 N Halsted St, Chicago, 773-477-9189
www.sidetrackchicago.com
NEIGHBORHOOD: Lakeview
A large gay video bar with five different bar areas on
two-levels including a deck bar. Show tunes on the
big screen, sing-along nights. Friendly crowd and
staff.

THE VIOLET HOUR
1520 N Damen Ave, Chicago, 773-252-1500
www.theviolethour.com
NEIGHBORHOOD: Wicker Park
This cocktail lounge may be difficult to find as there's no sign but it's worth the search. Inside there's a sign requesting that you refrain from using your cell phone. The décor is interesting with crystal chandeliers and beautiful hardwood floors giving the space a ballroom feel. The classic cocktails served are delish and strong but slow to come as the bartenders take great care in the preparation. Great atmosphere for drinking with friends.

WEEGEE'S LOUNGE
3659 W Armitage Ave, Chicago, 773-384-0707
www.weegeeslounge.com
NEIGHBORHOOD: Logan Square
An old-school cocktail lounge that does things their way, like making their own sour mix and ginger syrup. Here you'll find an impressive menu of beers (more than 100) with many coming from small brewers. The bar is known for its glamorous, yet potent cocktails like the Aviation made from gin, fresh lemon juice, crème de violette and Luxardo maraschino liqueur. The bar also serves classic tunes ranging from Glenn Miller to Memphis Slim.

INDEX

OTHER BOOKS BY THE FOOD ENTHUSIAST
That you will thoroughly enjoy

Austin
Barcelona
Buenos Aires
Cape Cod
Charleston
Chicago
Fort Lauderdale
Houston
Key West & the Florida Keys
Las Vegas
Los Angeles
Memphis
Miami & South Beach
Montreal
Nashville
New Orleans
New York / Brooklyn
New York / Downtown
New York / Manhattan
Downtown – Midtown - Upper East Side - Upper West Side
New York / Midtown
Orlando / Central Florida
Portland (Ore.)
San Diego
San Francisco
Savannah
Toronto

26010929R00048

Made in the USA
San Bernardino, CA
16 November 2015